My Dad Builds The Internet

My Dad Builds The Internet

This is me,
And this is my dad.

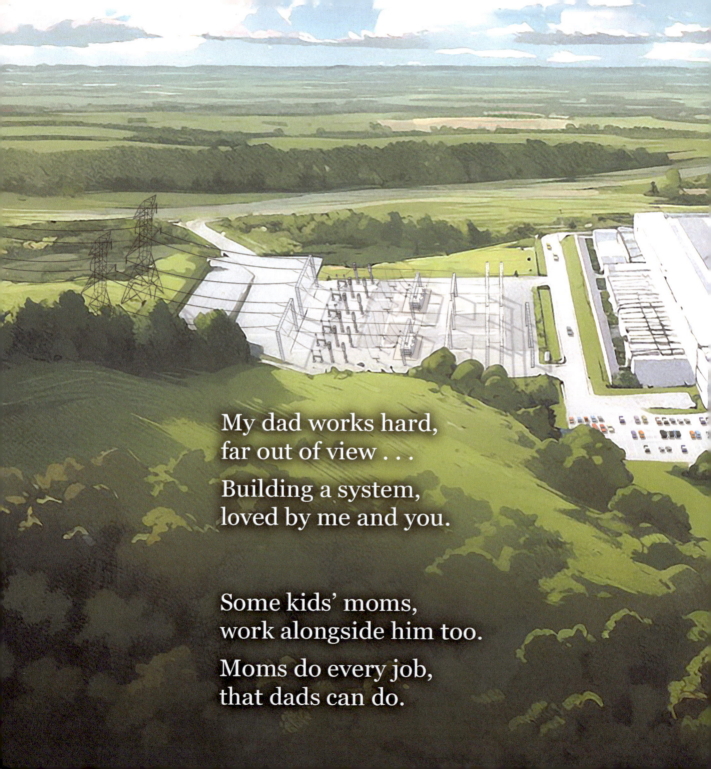

My dad works hard,
far out of view . . .

Building a system,
loved by me and you.

Some kids' moms,
work alongside him too.

Moms do every job,
that dads can do.

It's no secret,
the internet connects us all.

From connecting with friends,
to Grandma's loving calls.

From sharing photos,
and navigating maps . . .

To sending X-rays,
along healing paths.

But what *is* a secret,
that many don't know:

When the internet's off duty,
where does it go?

How could something so big,
not have a home?

In fact it lives,
just outside of town . . .

Where giant servers,
hum from sunup to sundown.

They connect to cities,
through cables underground . . .

As the internet's superhighway,
circling the whole world 'round.

So when we send photos straight to the cloud . . . Offloaded from our phones, but not too far to be found . . .

It's Dad's data center we trust,
to keep 'em safe and sound.

Or toy shopping,
reading online reviews . . .

Or flying to see family,
which flight to choose . . .

Dad's data center,
gives that digital boost.

Yet from the outside,
Dad works in a boring facility.

But peek inside his hive,
to find it buzzing with activity.

Brilliant men and women,
work around the clock tirelessly . . .

Keeping the whole world,
at our fingertips wirelessly.

So tomorrow let's look around,
at everything so essential. . .

Made possible by my dad,
and the internet's unlimited potential.

Until then . . .

Good night to the internet,
Circling 'round the earth . . .

Built by my dad,
and thousands more . . .

Who all love their kids,
so much that it hurts.

—The End—

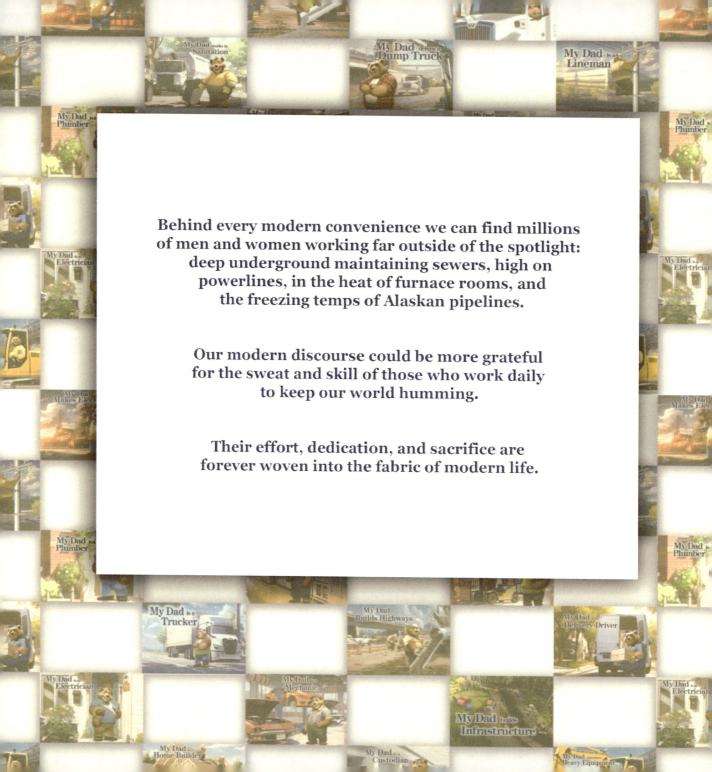

Behind every modern convenience we can find millions of men and women working far outside of the spotlight: deep underground maintaining sewers, high on powerlines, in the heat of furnace rooms, and the freezing temps of Alaskan pipelines.

Our modern discourse could be more grateful for the sweat and skill of those who work daily to keep our world humming.

Their effort, dedication, and sacrifice are forever woven into the fabric of modern life.

MEET MORE OF THE BEAR TRADES CREW!

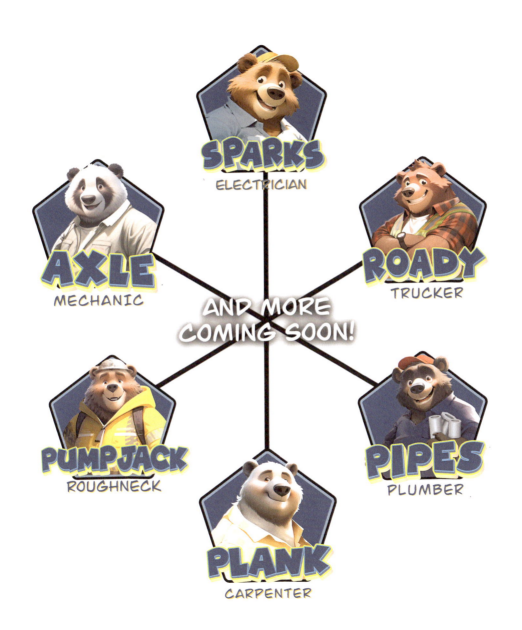

SPARKS
ELECTRICIAN

AXLE
MECHANIC

ROADY
TRUCKER

AND MORE
COMING SOON!

PUMP JACK
ROUGHNECK

PIPES
PLUMBER

PLANK
CARPENTER

www.ingramcontent.com/pod-product-compliance
Lightning Source LLC
LaVergne TN
LVRC091719070326
832904LV00037B/308